It's Earth Day

by John Manos

Table of Contents

Earth Day

environment

planet

pollution

projects

recycle

What Is Earth Day?

What is your favorite day of the year? Is your birthday your favorite day? You know that people care about you on that day. People might give a party for you.

Earth Day is like a birthday for Earth! On Earth Day, people think about our **planet**. People show that they care about Earth. They teach others to care, too.

▲ Do you make birthday cards to give? A child made this card for Earth Day.

Earth Day is on April 22 each year in most places. Earth Day is on the first day of spring in other places. That day is March 20 or March 21.

People all around the world have fun on Earth Day. People think of ways to help keep Earth clean and beautiful.

Did You Know?

- In 1990, millions of people celebrated Earth Day.
- Today, at least 140 nations around the world celebrate Earth Day.

◀ April 22 is Earth Day. People plant trees to help Earth.

Before Earth Day, many people did not worry about Earth. People thought our planet would always be safe and clean. Earth is so big! What could hurt Earth?

▲ The smoke from this factory can hurt Earth.

Dirty gases in the air could hurt Earth. Trash in the water could hurt Earth. **Pollution** could hurt Earth. In 1970, newspapers told about pollution in many places on Earth.

In Their Own Words

The person who started Earth Day said that everyone should

"wake up and do something."

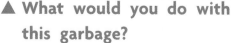

▲ What would you do with this garbage?

Pollution was a big problem. What could solve the problem? A group of people had an idea. Everyone could celebrate Earth and learn about Earth's problems on the same day. The group of people started Earth Day.

▲ The first Earth Day celebration was on April 22, 1970.

The first Earth Day was a success! On that day, people wanted to learn about Earth's problems. People came together to learn about the **environment**. People wanted to protect Earth from pollution. They wanted to learn how to solve the problems.

▲ These people are telling others about Earth's problems.

What Do People Do on Earth Day?

On Earth Day, people want to do something. One problem is too much garbage. People decide to make less garbage. They do not throw away their papers, bottles, and cans. People **recycle** this kind of trash.

▲ Do you recycle paper, plastic, and glass?

People put the paper, bottles, and cans in a recycling bin. This trash goes to a factory. The paper, bottles, and cans become new products.

People discover how to solve some of Earth's problems on Earth Day. When people recycle, they are helping to solve Earth's problems!

▲ Do you know this symbol? You can help Earth when you use products with this symbol.

What do kids around the world do on Earth Day? Kids made these plans for Earth Day.

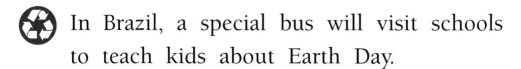 In Brazil, a special bus will visit schools to teach kids about Earth Day.

In Nigeria, over 10,000 kids will start clean-up **projects**.

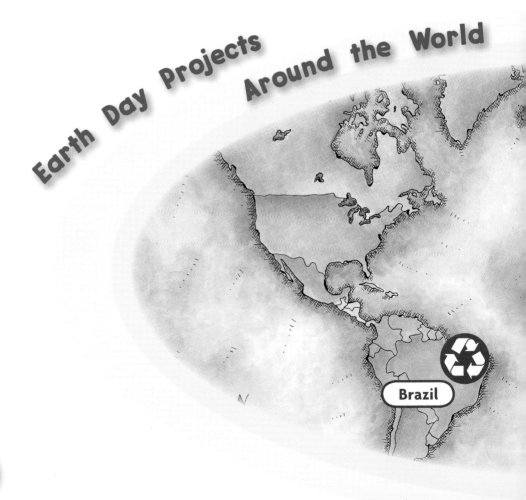

Earth Day Projects Around the World

Brazil

In Poland, 10,000 people will pick up trash where they live.

 In India, students will plant 3,000 trees.

These kids are really doing something for Earth Day!

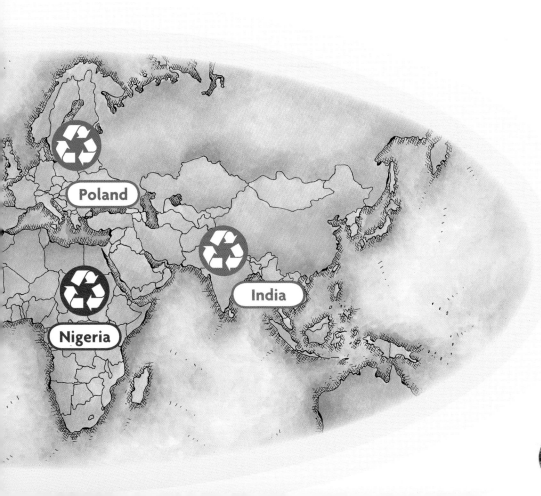

Who Does Important Projects?

The president gives awards to kids on Earth Day. The awards honor kids who did Earth Day projects. The president chooses ten projects each year. Each project helps Earth in a different way. The president gives each kid the President's Environmental Youth Award.

▲ These kids won awards. They met with President Bush.

This Project Was a Winner!

Kids at Central Elementary School wanted to stop pollution. Why did these kids win an award?

Before the Project	After the Project
People did not recycle many cans.	People recycled many more cans.
Kids threw shoes in the garbage.	Kids collected 286 pairs of shoes. Other kids used the shoes.
Kids threw trash in the garbage.	Kids used some trash to make artwork. They sold the artwork and gave money to the school.

How Can You Help Earth?

Earth Day reminds you to take care of Earth. You take care of Earth when you recycle paper. You protect Earth when you make less trash. Some kids learn what their town will do for Earth Day. Other kids plan an Earth Day party.

You can make an invitation for Earth Day.

PLANT A TREE

Where: in front of 55 West Street
Date: April 22
Time: 2:00 P.M.

Celebrate Earth Day!

Learn how to plant and care for a tree. Bring a piece of yarn.

Neighbors can show how to make a garden. Other neighbors can show how to plant trees. Grown-ups and kids can hang yarn on the branches. The yarn is a way of saying welcome to the tree. Birds will use the yarn for their nests. You are saying welcome to the birds, too.

▲ The kids in this parade are honoring Earth Day.

What will you do on the next Earth Day? Will you learn about Earth's problems? Will you plant a tree? You can do a green project. When you recycle trash, you are doing a green project. A green project helps the environment.

Many people just say thank you to Earth. The people go outdoors and have fun. Some people sing songs. One song says that planet Earth is our only home!

Honor Earth

Learn about Earth

EARTH DAY

Do projects for Earth

Glossary

Earth Day (ERTH DAY): a day when we think about Earth's health. See page 4.

environment (in-VI-run-ment): everything around you, such as the air, water, and land See page 9.

planet (PLA-net): a heavenly body that circles the sun See page 4.

pollution (puh-LOO-shun): anything that makes the environment dirty See page 7.

projects (PRAH-jekts): planned activities See page 12.

recycle (ree-SI-kul): to process things so that they can be used again See page 10.

Index

20